D0852015

Dedication: for my very special friend, Heather Gibbons – a truly wonderful little person! Lots of love and thousands of thank you's, from Juliette.

First published in Great Britain in 1991.
Published simultaneously by Exley Publications Ltd, 16 Chalk Hill, Watford, Herts WD1 4BN, United Kingdom and Exley Giftbooks, 359 East Main Street, Suite 3D, Mount Kisco, NY 10549, USA.

Second third and fourth printings 1992
Fifth printing 1993
Sixth printing 1994

Copyright © Exley Publications, 1991
Selection © Helen Exley
Edited: Helen Exley
Illustrations: Juliette Clarke

ISBN 1-85015-274-8

Printed and bound in Hungary.

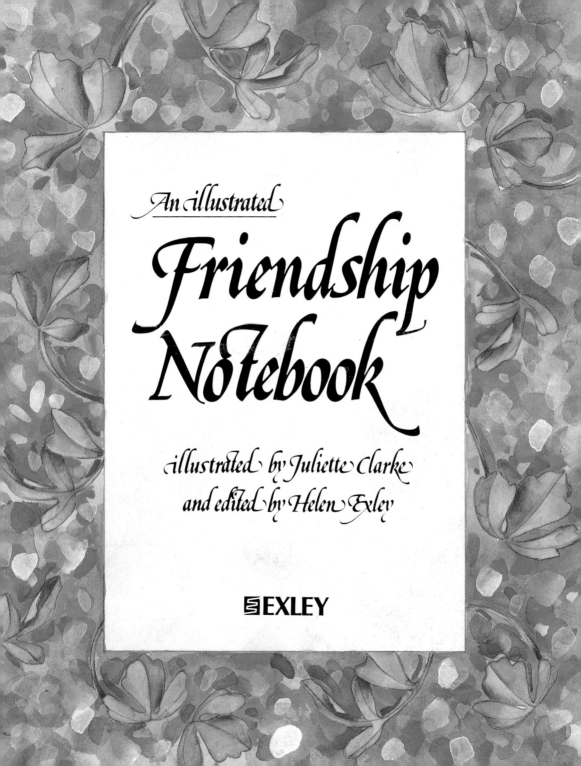

An illustrated

Friendship Notebook

illustrated by Juliette Clarke
and edited by Helen Exley

EXLEY

What do we live for, if it is not to make life less difficult for each other?
Mary Ann Evans (George Eliot) (1819-1880)

A *phone call is good. But you can re-read a letter.*

Pam Brown, b.1928

Guard within yourself that treasure, kindness.
Know how to give without hesitation,
how to lose without regret,
how to acquire without meanness.
Know how to replace in your heart,
by the happiness of those you love,
the happiness you may be wanting yourself.

George Sand (1804-1876)

Friendship, although incredibly sensitive to mood and need, is apparently blind to appearances.
Schoolfriends — skinny, spotty, besotted with ballet and palominos — see no change in each other, forty years on.
Pam Brown, b.1928

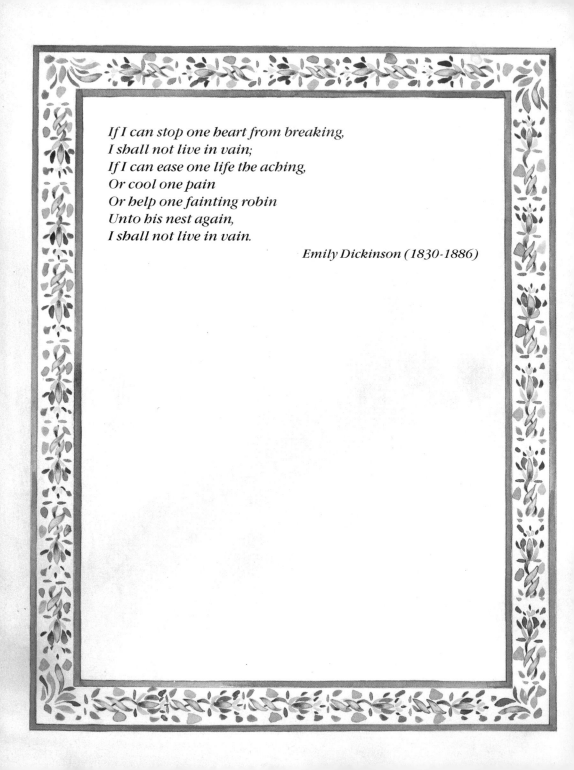

If I can stop one heart from breaking,
I shall not live in vain;
If I can ease one life the aching,
Or cool one pain
Or help one fainting robin
Unto his nest again,
I shall not live in vain.

Emily Dickinson (1830-1886)

Whoever is happy will make others happy too.
Anne Frank (1929-1945)

That best portion of a good man's life, His little, nameless, unremembered acts of kindness and of love.

William Wordsworth (1770-1850)

*Friendship is always a sweet
responsibility, never an opportunity.*
Kahlil Gibran (1883-1931)

There's nothing worth the wear of winning, but laughter and the love of friends.

Hilaire Belloc (1870-1953)

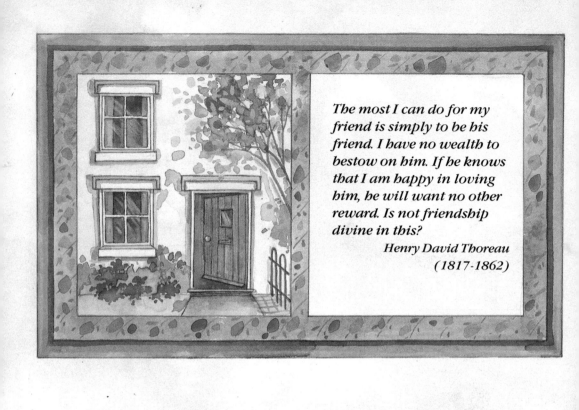

The most I can do for my friend is simply to be his friend. I have no wealth to bestow on him. If he knows that I am happy in loving him, he will want no other reward. Is not friendship divine in this?

Henry David Thoreau
(1817-1862)

Each friend represents a world in us, a world possibly not born until they arrive, and it is only by this meeting that a new world is born.

Anaïs Nin (1903-1977)

The world is full of friends waiting to meet you.

Marion C. Garretty, b. 1917

A friendship can weather most things and thrive in thin soil – but it needs a little mulch of letters and phonecalls and small silly presents every so often – just to save it from drying out completely.

Pam Brown, b.1928

*True happiness consists not in
the multitude of friends,
But in the worth and choice.*
Ben Jonson (1572-1637)

Friends choose each other, try each other out, don't have to go too fast at first, don't have to promise to have lunch every day from now to eternity.

Margaret Mead
(1901-1978)

The thread of our life would be dark,
Heaven knows!
If it were not with friendship and love
intertwin'd.
Thomas Moore (1779-1852)

For whoever knows how to return a
kindness he has received must be a
friend above all price.
Sophocles (469-406 B.C.)

There is no friend like an old friend
Who has shared our morning days,
No greeting like his welcome,
No homage like his praise.
Fame is the scentless flower,
With gaudy crown of gold;
But friendship is the breathing rose,
With sweets in every fold.

Oliver Wendell Holmes (1809-1894)

If someone has given you a joy
or hope or an idea that
transforms your thinking—<u>tell</u>
them, however important they
are. Simply. Quietly.
You may well brighten a very
dark day.
Helen Thomson, b. 1943

Respect. . . is appreciation of the <u>separateness</u> of the other person, of the ways in which he or she is unique.

Annie Gottlieb

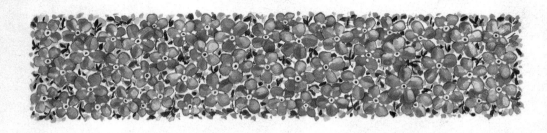

A friend is a present which you give yourself.
Robert Louis Stevenson (1850-1894)

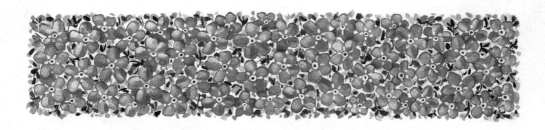

Hold a true friend with both your hands.

Nigerian Proverb

I love you not only for what you are, but for what I am when I am with you. I love you not only for what you have made of yourself, but for what you are making of me.

Mary Ann Evans (George Eliot) (1819-1880)

May friendship, like wine, improve as time advances,
And may we always have old wine, old friends, and
young cares.

Author Unknown

The cheapest of all things is kindness, its exercise requiring the least possible trouble and self-sacrifice.

Samuel Smiles (1812-1904)

A friend may well be reckoned the masterpiece of nature.
Ralph Waldo Emerson (1803-1882)

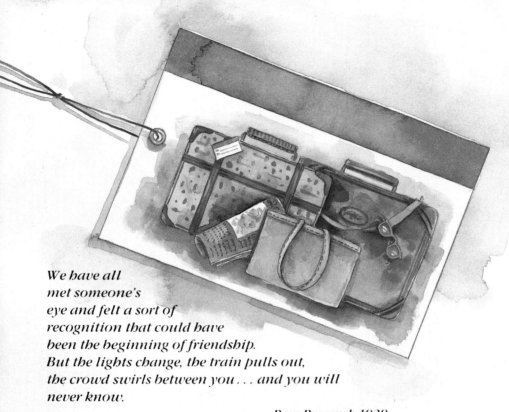

*We have all
met someone's
eye and felt a sort of
recognition that could have
been the beginning of friendship.
But the lights change, the train pulls out,
the crowd swirls between you . . . and you will
never know.*

Pam Brown, b.1928

Once there was a king who felt exceedingly unhappy because he thought there were no really good people left in his kingdom. So he said to a famous artist, "Paint me a picture of a really good person". The artist did so and the king was delighted. He stood back to admire the portrait and suddenly realized that all the features were familiar. He recognised the brow of his priest, and the happy eyes of his minstrel, the lips of his small daughter, the lovely smile of his beloved wife, and so on.

The moral of the story being, of course, that there is no completely good person — but all the people round us have qualities to be admired.

Francis Gay

Do not keep the alabaster boxes of your love and tenderness sealed up until your friends are dead. Fill their lives with sweetness. Speak approving cheering words while their ears can hear them and while their hearts can be thrilled by them.

George W. Childs

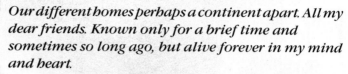

Our different homes perhaps a continent apart. All my dear friends. Known only for a brief time and sometimes so long ago, but alive forever in my mind and heart.

Helen Thomson, b.1943

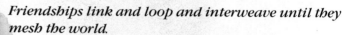

Friendships link and loop and interweave until they mesh the world.

Pam Brown, b.1928

Wishing to be friends is quick work, but friendship is a slow-ripening fruit.

Aristotle (384-322 B.C.)

The idea of strictly minding our own business is mouldy rubbish. Who could be so selfish?

Myrtie Barker

Yet "old friends" always seemed a contradiction to me. Age
cannot wither nor custom stale the infinite variety of friends
who, as long as you know them, remain as vibrant and
stimulating as the day you first met them.

Author Unknown

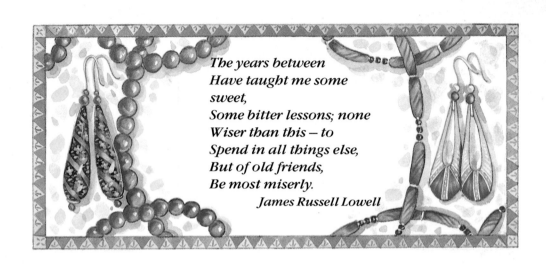

The years between
Have taught me some
sweet,
Some bitter lessons; none
Wiser than this — to
Spend in all things else,
But of old friends,
Be most miserly.
            James Russell Lowell

*How life
catches up with
us and teaches us to
love and forgive each other.*
Judy Collins, b.1939

You can't fake listening. It shows.

Raquel Welch, b.1942

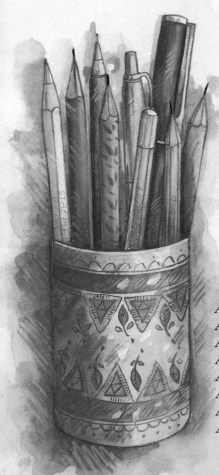

A little more kindness, a little less creed,
A little more giving, a little less greed,
A little more smile, a little less frown,
A little less kicking a man when he's down,
A little more "we", and a little less "I",
A little more laugh, a little less cry,
A little more flowers on the pathway of life,
And fewer on graves at the end of the strife.

                                        Anonymous

Wise sayings often fall on barren ground; but a kind word is never thrown away.

Sir Arthur Helps (1813-1875)

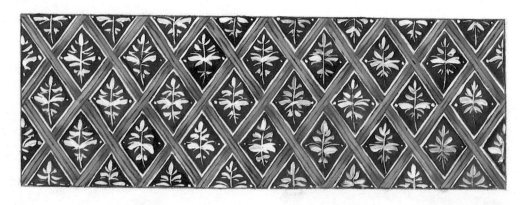

Friendship is unnecessary, like philosophy, like art. . . . It has no survival value; rather it is one of those things that give value to survival.

C. S. Lewis (1898-1963)

Paboos

Ju

Old friends are best. King James used to call for his old shoes; they were easiest for his feet.

John Seldon (1584-1654)

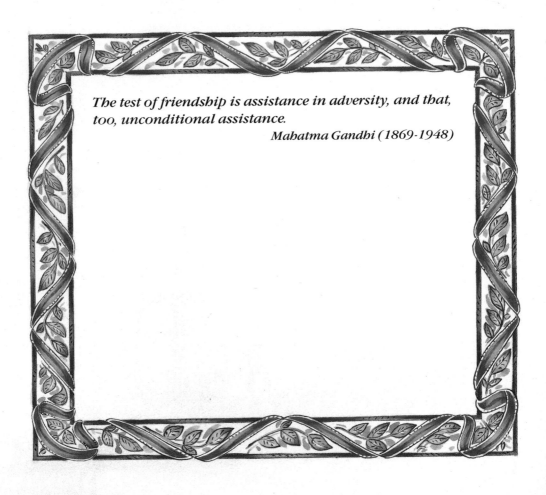

The test of friendship is assistance in adversity, and that, too, unconditional assistance.

Mahatma Gandhi (1869-1948)

Effua put her hand on my cheek: "Sister, you have need of a sister-friend because you need to weep and you need someone to watch you while you weep".

Maya Angelou, b.1928

Juliette Clarke

Friends, books, a cheerful heart, and conscience clear are the most choice companions we have here.

William Mather

*It is very easy to forgive others their mistakes;
it takes more grit and gumption to forgive
them for having witnessed your own.*

                    Jessamyn West, b. 1902

Happiness seems made to be shared.

Jean Racine (1639-1699)

I no doubt deserved my enemies, but I don't believe I deserved my friends.

Walt Whitman (1819-1892)

Don't walk in front of me,
I may not follow.
Don't walk behind me,
I may not lead.
Walk beside me,
And just be my friend.

Author Unknown